ARCHAEOLOGISTS DIG FOR CLUES

BY KATE DUKE

HarperCollins*Publishers*

Special thanks to Dan Rogers at the Smithsonian Institution,
to Drs. Elizabeth Graham and Peter Storck at the Royal Ontario Museum,
to Liz Hausen at the Center for American Archaeology,
and to the Archaeology Department at the University of Connecticut

The *Let's-Read-and-Find-Out Science* book series was originated by Dr. Franklyn M. Branley, Astronomer Emeritus and former Chairman of the American Museum–Hayden Planetarium, and was formerly co-edited by him and Dr. Roma Gans, Professor Emeritus of Childhood Education, Teachers College, Columbia University. Text and illustrations for each of the books in the series are checked for accuracy by an expert in the relevant field. For more information about Let's-Read-and-Find-Out Science books, please write to HarperCollins Children's Books, 10 East 53rd Street, New York, NY 10022.

HarperCollins®, ♣®, and Let's-Read-and-Find-Out Science® are trademarks of HarperCollins Publishers Inc.

Library of Congress Cataloging-in-Publication Data
Duke, Kate.
  Archaeologists dig for clues / by Kate Duke.
    p.   cm. — (Let's-read-and-find-out science. Stage 2)
    ISBN 0-06-027056-X. — ISBN 0-06-027057-8 (lib. bdg.)
    ISBN 0-06-445175-5 (pbk.)
    1. Archaeology—Juvenile literature.   I. Title.   II. Series.
CC171.D85   1997   95-10684
930—dc20   CIP
                                        AC

Typography by Elynn Cohen
1   2   3   4   5   6   7   8   9   10
❖
First Edition

ARCHAEOLOGISTS DIG FOR CLUES

On our summer vacation we got to go on a dig with our friend Sophie. She's a scientist—an archaeologist. She hunts for places where people once lived. Over time these places have gotten buried. Sophie digs them up. It's called excavating. She found a good place to excavate near where we lived.

4

The dig was in a cornfield. The farmers who owned the field had uncovered some prehistoric spear points with their plow. When she saw the points, Sophie asked for permission to hunt for more clues.

HOW DO YOU KNOW IT'S NOT AN ARROWHEAD?

BECAUSE IT'S MUCH TOO BIG!

PREHISTORIC HUNTERS USED SPEARS FOR THOUSANDS OF YEARS BEFORE THE BOW AND ARROW WERE EVEN INVENTED.

spear point

arrowhead (much smaller)

How do archaeologists decide where to dig?

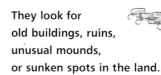

They look at things that builders, farmers, sometimes even animals have uncovered accidentally.

They look for old buildings, ruins, unusual mounds, or sunken spots in the land.

They look at pictures of the land taken from airplanes. These can show where old roads or walls were.

They look at old books and maps for clues to buried sites.

Sophie showed us the test pits she had dug to test the ground for other interesting buried stuff. In some of the pits she had found more spear points. They were in a layer of dirt that was darker than the dirt above it. The dark earth was important. It was a sign that people had lived on that spot long ago.

WHY DOES THE GROUND PEOPLE LIVE ON TURN DARK?

BECAUSE PEOPLE HAVE WALKED ON IT, COOKED ON IT, SPILLED THINGS, BURNED THINGS, SPIT, PEED, THROWN UP. . . .

IN OTHER WORDS, THE DIRT GETS DIRTY!

UGH! MY POOR SNEAKERS!

Sophie needed to know how old the dig site was. So she sent some pieces of burned wood from the dark-dirt layer to the archaeology lab. A carbon-dating test, which measured chemicals in the wood, showed that it was six thousand years old!

That meant the people who had burned the wood in their campfires had lived in the Archaic Era. We didn't know too much about that time period, but we figured we'd find out once we got to the dig.

OF COURSE, ARCHAEOLOGISTS DON'T STUDY ONLY ANCIENT TIMES.

SOMEDAY ARCHAEOLOGISTS OF THE FUTURE WILL STUDY US!

I'M SURE THEY'LL FIND US VERY ATTRACTIVE.

Wow! That's really old!

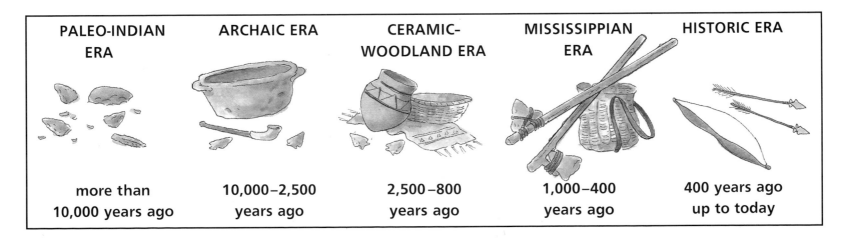

PALEO-INDIAN ERA	ARCHAIC ERA	CERAMIC-WOODLAND ERA	MISSISSIPPIAN ERA	HISTORIC ERA
more than 10,000 years ago	10,000–2,500 years ago	2,500–800 years ago	1,000–400 years ago	400 years ago up to today

Archaeologists always dig square holes. That's because they're scientists. Their digging is scientific digging—neat and organized. And being organized makes it easier for them to keep records of where they make each find.

How Do Things Get Buried So Far Down?

When something is left on the ground, day after day, year after year, leaves fall on it,

dust blows onto it,

rain washes dirt over it. . . .

Little by little, bit by bit, it gets covered up. After thousands of years, it can be buried pretty deep.

We couldn't wait to do a little scientific digging ourselves. Maybe we'd excavate some buried treasure! Or an underground tomb! Or a mummy!

But when we looked at the stuff Sophie had already collected, we were confused. There were a couple of spear points, but the rest just looked like a bunch of rocks and pebbles and dirt. It sure didn't look like treasure.

That was when we discovered the truth about archaeology.

The truth was a shock. Archaeologists hardly ever find treasure. They aren't even trying to! They're interested in the ordinary things that belonged to ordinary people. They even care about the stuff that people of the past dropped, or lost, or threw away. In other words, garbage. Archaeologists love ancient garbage!

They even have a special name for it—midden. When they study it and test it, they can find out all kinds of things about the people it once belonged to. So archaeologists are more like detectives than treasure hunters. They're trying to uncover the whole story of how people lived in the past, as truly as they can.

I WANT TO KNOW **EVERYTHING** ABOUT THE PEOPLE I STUDY.

WHAT DID THEY EAT? WHAT DID THEY WEAR?

WHAT WAS THEIR ENVIRONMENT LIKE?

HOW LONG DID THEY LIVE? WHAT DID THEY DIE OF?

WHAT DID THEY DO ALL DAY?

GEE, ARCHAEOLOGISTS ARE KIND OF NOSY.

What Would Your Garbage Tell About You?

Average kid's wastebasket

not so good in math

has crush on S.P.

has birthday June 3

has really big feet

drinks banana soda

has cool clothes

eats too much chocolate

is a little messy

Bones and shells from this area show that people ate:

deer
muskrat
fox
beaver
duck
goose
quail
turkey
clams
oysters
turtles
pigeons
fish
snails

So Sophie's dirt wasn't just dirt. It had bits of six-thousand-year-old Archaic garbage in it. There were little pieces of bones and shells. They showed what animals the Archaic people hunted. And even littler specks of black charcoal showed what plants they ate. Those specks once had been seeds and nutshells. They had fallen into the fire and burned while being roasted for somebody's dinner, one day thousands of years ago.

Some of the many plants these Archaic people ate were:

hickory nuts
acorns
pecans
chestnuts
pigweed
sunflower seeds
marsh elder
walnuts

They sure had plenty to eat.

No junk food, either!

THIS PIECE OF BONE SHOWS THE MARKS WHERE SOMEONE'S KNIFE SLICED OFF THE MEAT.

COOL!

YUM!

dirt

charcoal

cut marks

14

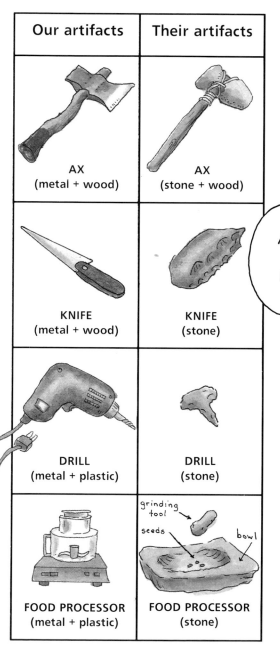

Our artifacts	Their artifacts
AX (metal + wood)	AX (stone + wood)
KNIFE (metal + wood)	KNIFE (stone)
DRILL (metal + plastic)	DRILL (stone)
FOOD PROCESSOR (metal + plastic)	FOOD PROCESSOR (stone)

grinding tool
seeds
bowl

Sophie's rocks weren't just rocks, either. They were artifacts. An artifact is a thing—anything at all—that people have made. Someone in Archaic times had turned those rocks into artifacts by making them into tools and weapons.

Stone flakes
are artifacts, too!

15

Artifacts and midden are clues to the past. And like detectives at a crime scene, archaeologists at a dig try not to break or disturb anything that might be evidence. They use tools that can excavate finds gently. And they never ever take a find away from the dig without first marking down exactly where it came from. Knowing *where* something was found can help explain *why* it was there and *what* it was used for.

stone knives

Finally we were ready to start digging. Sophie gave us each a teeny little trowel to work with. No shovels! Archeologists use tools that can excavate artifacts gently. She told us to scrape the dirt up lightly, taking off only the tiniest layer at a time.

After that, we learned how to screen the dirt we'd collected, to be sure we hadn't missed any tiny artifacts or midden.

ONE-TWO! CHA-CHA-CHA! SCREENING IS FUN!

GOOD EXERCISE, TOO!

Large pieces are caught on screen.

Smaller bits fall through.

PUT ALL THE DIRT YOU COLLECT INTO THIS BUCKET.

THIS IS THE SLOWEST WAY TO DIG I EVER HEARD OF!

WHOOSH!

HEY! I'M NOT AN ARTIFACT!

An air pump blows away dirt without even touching the artifact.

Metal and bamboo picks can get grains of dirt out of nooks and crannies.

YOUR DENTIST USES THESE.

scoop made from milk jug

Soft brushes can sweep away dirt without scratching.

We held it in our hands and thought about how no one had touched it for all those thousands of years, until now.

Next we found a row of dark spots on the ground. We didn't think they were important. But Sophie did. She knew right away that they were marks left by the wooden posts that had held up an Archaic person's house. We wondered if spots could be artifacts too. But Sophie said a find like this is called a feature.

20

A feature is like an artifact, because it's something made by people; but it's also a place. Roads, buildings, swimming pools, cemeteries, and parking lots are all features. Archaeologists like finding features because they're good clues to where things happened. Our feature—the posthole spots—told us where a family had once lived.

BUT HOW DO WE EXCAVATE THEM? THEY'RE PART OF THE GROUND.

WE'LL JUST TAKE A SAMPLE OF THE STAINED EARTH.

SIGH!

How to Build an Archaic House

1. Set thin tree trunks in a circle.

2. Bend them to make a frame.

3. Cover with grass mats.

4. Move in.

The next thing we worked on was the coolest of all. It was a grave. With a skeleton in it—a dog skeleton. A pebble with a hole drilled in it lay by the dog's neck, and under the skeleton there was charcoal from a fire. We wondered if the pebble had once hung on a collar, and why the dog had been buried in the ashes. It was mysterious and spooky to think about.

Excavating a skeleton is tricky. You can't let any of the bones move out of place. Sophie showed us a special way to do it.

NICE DRAWING.

It was late when we finished. Time to stop digging, Sophie said, but not to stop working. We measured our finds, and drew them, and photographed them, and bagged them, and labeled them.

Archaic Site
Square J1
Level 1

NICE POOCHIE.

POOCHIE?

ruler shows the size of object in photo

Artifact Bag
(just a plain bag)

ARCHAIC SITE
July 24, 1996
Square 4.D
Level 1

awl

vial to prevent breaking

HOW DO I LOOK?

NOT AS GOOD AS THESE POSTHOLE SPOTS!

Archaic Site
Square J1
Level 1

water to darken stain for photo

Next, Sophie handed us all clipboards and pencils. We were finding out fast that archaeology isn't just excavating. You have to be as careful about keeping records as you are about digging. We wrote down exactly what we'd found and exactly where we'd found it.

Sophie marked everything on the archaeological map she was making of the whole dig. When we looked at it, we could see why it mattered *where* you found stuff as much as what the stuff was. Every square on the map matched a square in the dig. The map showed us that our house had been part of a tiny village. We saw where each house had been, and where the villagers had cooked their food, and made their tools, and dumped their garbage.

I SEE OUR DOG GRAVE!

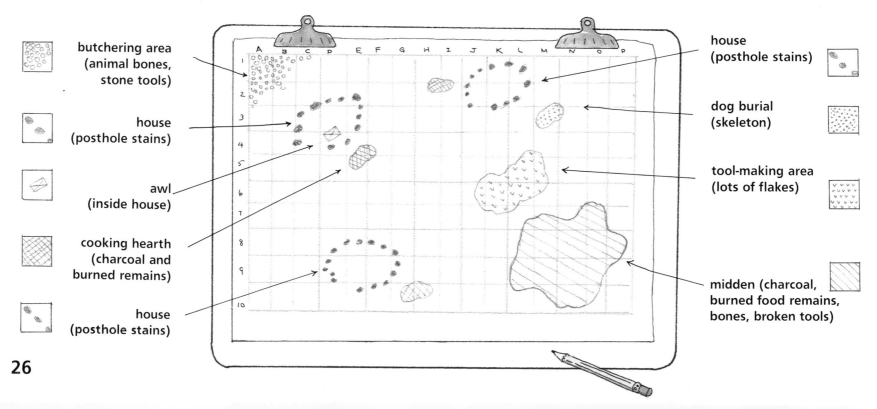

butchering area (animal bones, stone tools)

house (posthole stains)

awl (inside house)

cooking hearth (charcoal and burned remains)

house (posthole stains)

house (posthole stains)

dog burial (skeleton)

tool-making area (lots of flakes)

midden (charcoal, burned food remains, bones, broken tools)

The map made it easy to imagine what the village might have looked like. It was a picture put together from the tiniest clues—specks of dirt, and stones, and bones. We thought it was good detective work.

We helped Sophie count the bags from our dig to make sure none had been left behind. We wet-screened samples of dirt, and cleaned artifacts, and measured them, and put them into plastic bags, and labeled them.

Wet-Screening Dirt

1. Sprinkle dirt over a pot of water.
2. Sand and dirt sink.
3. Fish scales, charcoal, etc. float.
4. Very fine screen scoops "floaters" up.

REMEMBER WHAT THIS IS?

toothbrush

plain water

card identifying artifact

drying rack for artifacts

25, 26, 27...

Last of all, we entered all the facts about them into a computer. Our finds would never get lost, that was for sure. Now Sophie and her team could study them together with the other clues from the dig. And maybe get some answers to their questions about what it was like to live in Archaic times.

We'd done a lot of hard work. But we were ready for more tomorrow. There are all kinds of archeological clues out there, just waiting to be discovered. And you never know what you might find in one square hole!

What do you do if you find something in your backyard or wherever?

Check one:

○ Grab a shovel! Start digging! Mess up the site, mix up the dirt, break artifacts left and right!

○ Show your find to an expert at a museum or local archaeological society. Bring a map to show exactly where you found it. Or call your state archaeologists. If they decide to do a dig, you might get to watch, or even help out.

DIRT, BEAUTIFUL DIRT!